Dear Stuart,

Thanks for your help in making ShopHorror.
Page 133, Herr Flick, is the first photo taken
with your camera.

Guy.

4th

# OPEN

## HOURS OF BUSINESS

| | A.M. | P.M. | | A.M. | P.M. |
|---|---|---|---|---|---|
| Monday | 8.00 | 5.30 | Thursday | 8.00 | 1.00 |
| Tuesday | 8.00 | 5.30 | Friday | 8.00 | 5.30 |
| Wednesday | 8.00 | 5.30 | Saturday | 9.00 | 5.30 |
| Lunch | | | Sunday | | |

# SHOP HORROR
## The Best of the Worst in British Shop Names

GUY SWILLINGHAM

First published in Great Britain in 2005 by Fourth Estate
An imprint of HarperCollinsPublishers
77–85 Fulham Palace Road, London W6 8JB
www.4thestate.co.uk

Copyright © Guy Swillingham 2005

1 3 5 7 9 10 8 6 4 2

The right of Guy Swillingham to be identified as the author of this work has been
asserted by him in accordance with the Copyright, Designs and Patents Act 1988

A catalogue record for this book is available from the British Library

ISBN 0-00-719813-2

Printed by Proost

## THANKS AND ACKNOWLEDGEMENTS

A big 'Thank you' goes to these people for their help and support in turning
Shop Horror from an idea into reality.

Alan, Kathy and Molly for all their love and encouragement. Lee and Stuart
for their suggestions and support. Amber for being shop-finder, navigator,
caterer, whip-cracker, themed list-maker, travelling onion, ground control
and monkey love. Nicholas Pearson, Silvia Crompton and Julian Humphries
at Fourth Estate for their guidance, and Nick Davies for opening the door.

To everyone who suggested their favourite shops, thank you. Please keep
them coming.

A special mention goes to the truly inventive shopkeepers whose businesses
feature in this book. I know you get it. Please don't sue.

This book is dedicated to the memory of Clare, forever.

# SHOP HORROR

There is a menace lurking in the streets of Britain. It is not drugs. It is not crime. It is not loitering teen gangs. It is something far more threatening. Something that offends the decency of right-thinking people. Innocently going about their business, they are suddenly confronted by this horror. They stand petrified, not knowing whether to laugh or cry.

That menace is the shop with a pun-based name.

These attempts at store-front comedy lie scattered the length and breadth of this country. Their abuse of humour and language cause stomach-churning, cringe-inducing reactions whenever encountered.

There is much talk of cleaning up our streets. Shop Horror had had enough of talk. It was time to act. We scoured the land, rounding up the offending establishments to hold them up as a lesson to all.

Then something happened.

We realised that there comes a point when things get so bad, they're actually good. These were not just the UK's worst pun-based shop names. They were also the best. We knew then it was time to celebrate, not castigate, these wonderfully terrible stores by presenting them here.

Admission to this rogues' gallery is an honour. An honour which is never granted lightly. The Shop Horror panel has carefully assessed the most ridiculously named outlets in the country. It takes an indefinable combination of wit, ingenuity and sometimes pure stupidity to come up with an inspirational shop name. Only then will we admit it to this hall of name and shame.

Not only have we assembled the best of the worst in British shop names, in special cases we take you inside the stores to discover what lies beyond their humorous exteriors. We also reveal what happens when the world of retail collides with the realms of film, TV, music and others.

These shops do more than entertain, they help preserve our heritage. This nation of shopkeepers is being overrun by corporate chains in a homogenous High Street. By displaying their individual names, these stores are standing up for the independent retailer. Shop Horror is proud to record their efforts for posterity.

These funny businesses sometimes achieve local infamy. Now, for the first time ever, they are assembled in one place to be enjoyed or endured by the whole nation. Shop Horror invites you to join us on this window-shopping trip around the country. If you think these shops are funny, you will enjoy the ride. If you think they are terrible, treat this as aversion retail therapy. From the truly awful to the genuinely inventive, Shop Horror salutes them all.

*Guy Swillingham*

# SHOP HORROR

## The Best of the Worst in British Shop Names

### GUY SWILLINGHAM

Lanark, Lanarkshire

Twickenham, Middlesex

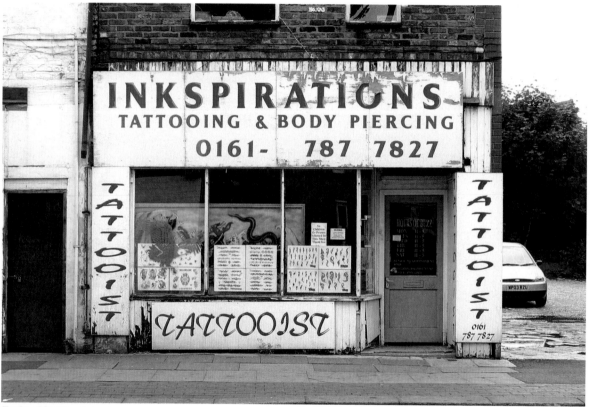

Eccles, Manchester

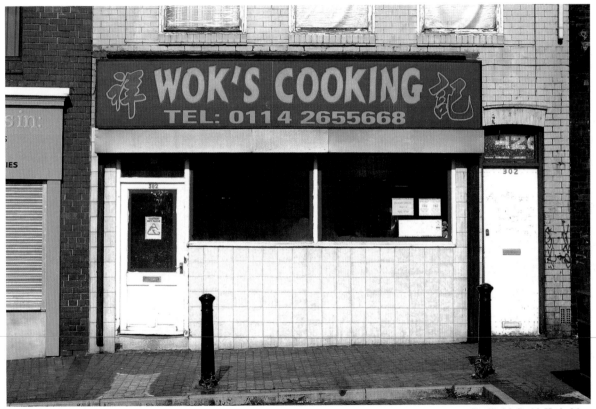

Sheffield, South Yorkshire

THE VINYL RESTING PLACE ☎ FAX
Est. 1994 081 656 3350 As Seen on T.V.

RECORDS
CDs & VIDEOS
45s

C.D.s & RECORDS
BOUGHT & SOLD

OPEN

BARBARA          CHRIS

Shirley, Croydon

*"Vinyl's best, absolutely, one hundred per cent. It's more sophisticated, more attractive. You've got the headphones on, listening to the record, looking at the sleeve. You notice so much more."*

BUY any 5 items get cheapest FREE

Just having tea, we were discussing it. All of a sudden, Barbara said, 'How about the Vinyl Resting Place?'

There's a zebra crossing outside. Drivers stop, look at the sign, it dawns on them. I like to see their reactions.

An orange vinyl version of ELO's 'Out of the Blue'. Nobody knew an orange one existed. It was normally black or blue vinyl. We didn't know what it was worth. In auction it went for £600.

*Mostly our stock comes from people who bring things in, but we also go to car-boot sales early in the morning and get muddy knees.*

I like comedy records. I'm looking for an album by a group called Cat's Arse. It's worth a fiver.
**Badger,** customer

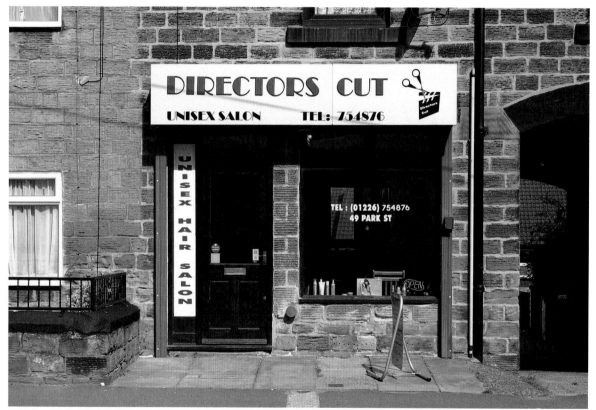

Wombwell, South Yorkshire

Tunbridge Wells, Kent

13

Hanwell, London

Westcliff-On-Sea, Essex

15

NICE BUNS BIG BAPS
01204 465556

OPEN

SUMMER SPECIAL
BACON BARM
£1.00

NICE BUNS
BIG BAPS
SANDWICHES AND
HOT FOODS

**JOANNE JONES**

Bolton, Lancashire

" *I was gonna call it 'Nice Buns' or 'Big Baps' and my sister said, 'Why not call it both?' So I did. It had to be something cheeky.* "

nice buns big baps
tel 01204 465556

The best dish? Hot Beef with onions and mushrooms, £2.
**Brian Bibby**

**DELICIOUS HOT SNACKS**

A. La Carte
Catering & Refrigeration
Equipment Ltd.
Tel./Fax. No: 01204 363121

| | |
|---|---|
| Water | 70p |
| milk | 50p |
| Fresh air - FREE | |
| small pop | 40p |
| Spring Water | 60p |

I like it so much here, I moved in next door!
**Martin Riley,** customer

A man came in and said that he heard of us in a caff in London. They said, 'If you ever go to Bolton, go to "Nice Buns Big Baps".' So he did.

Customers, they're like your mates. They come in and tell you their problems. We like to have a crack. I bar people you know 'n' all. Peter Kay's barred.

*People here are dead nice. Typical Northern people. It's like Coronation Street. You get so much support in here. I've had counselling sessions off two coppers in the back.*

| | | | |
|---|---|---|---|
| | £1.25 | £1.45 | Cold Sandwiches |
| | £1.50 | £1.70 | Salad |
| | £1.50 | £1.70 | Ham |
| Egg | £1.60 | £1.80 | Beef |
| | £1.70 | £1.90 | |
| | £1.50 | | |
| | £1.60 | | |

T BAGS  SUGAR

**NICE BUNS BIG BAPS**

SANDWICHES AND HOT FOOD

79 Raphael Street
Off Shepherd Cross Street
Halliwell
Bolton

Walkley, Sheffield

18

Mr G Swillingham
Shop Horror
High Street
London

**Battersea Dogs Home**
Patron: Her Majesty The Queen
President: His Royal Highness Prince Michael of Kent

4, Battersea Park Road, London SW8 4AA
Tel: 020-7622 3626    Fax: 020-7622 6451
www.dogshome.org

6th September 2004

Dear Mr Swillingham,

We at Battersea Dogs Home were not aware of the existence of the Sheffield fish and chips shop Battersea Cod's Home.

Now that it has been brought to our attention, we can state that we do not usually approve of the use of our name for other businesses or establishments. However, we were tickled by the light-hearted approach to the naming of this restaurant. Every bit of public awareness helps when we are trying to find the best possible homes for our dogs and cats.

We just hope that if the proprietors of Battersea Cods Home own a dog or a cat, that it came from us.

**❝ I don't own a dog. Or a cat. ❞**
IAN PRINGLE, OWNER, BATTERSEA COD'S HOME

Olivia Stanton
Communications Officer.

19

Waterloo, London

Newark-on-Trent, Nottinghamshire

21

It is widely thought that cinema's ultimate accolade is to be immortalised as a star on Hollywood's Walk of Fame. We at Shop Horror hold a different view. We believe the highest tribute is found not on an American sidewalk, but lining British pavements. For a film has no greater honour than to be the inspiration behind a UK shop name.

We present here the Shop Horror Cinema Top Ten. This, the first film chart not based on box-office takings, has been compiled by our expert panel. They have assessed the screams of horror and delight provoked by the following shops and the winners are...

# The Silver

**1** **Austin Flowers** Florist, Camden, London
**2** **Dye Hard** Hairdresser, Lincoln, Lincolnshire
**3** **Brief Encounter** Lingerie, Loughborough, Leicestershire
**4** **Goodfillas** Sandwiches, York, North Yorkshire

# Scream

**Honorable mentions...**

The Great Rack 'n' Rail Swindle — Clothing, Middlesborough, Co Durham

Filled of Dreams — Sandwiches, Beckenham, Kent

Barberella — Hairdresser, City Centre, Manchester

Eye Society — Optician, Bournemouth, Dorset

Catch 22 — Fishing tackle, Southport, Merseyside

The Wild Bunch — Florist, Bath, Avon

Blade Runner — Hairdresser, Ruddington, Nottinghamshire

5 **The Codfather** Fish & chips, Finchley, London

6 **A Fish Called Rhondda** Fish & chips, Ton Pentre, Rhondda Valley

7 **Blazing Saddles** Bicycles, Rustington, West Sussex

8 **Hello Deli** Delicatessen, Giffnock, Lanarkshire

9 **Hire Society** Dress hire, Middlesborough, Co Durham

10 **Facial Attraction** Beauty salon, Battersea, London

Peterborough, Cambridgeshire

Bourne, Lincolnshire

Leyland, Lancashire

St Neots, Cambridgeshire

SUITES, CARPETS & BEDS

SUITE SUCCESS Est 1992

SUITE SUCCESS

LEATHER SUITES
DIRECT

Entrance to
FURNITURE
BARGAINS
30 SUITES IN STOCK

FREE
DELIVERY
Within 30 mile radias

UP TO 70% OFF!

FREE LOCAL DELIVERY!

FREE LOCAL DELIVERY!

FREE LOCAL DELIVERY!

Metal and Pine beds on show upstairs

PHILIP EMERY

Port Talbot,
West Glamorgan

*My wife thought of it, basically. I told her I didn't want it to have anything to do with furniture or upholstery and she just came off the top of her head with 'Suite Success'.*

FREE DELIVERY ON ALL FURNITURE

(30 MILE RADIUS)

At the end of the day, we've got a motto which is 'Your success is our success'. You're successful buying the right product, and we're successful by selling. By making money, obviously.

*The most expensive suite? £1,499 in our shop. Solid oak frame, with leather upholstery. It's about £2,500 in most shops, but a lot cheaper with us. We're in the wrong end of town to charge high prices.*

You need to tell people what you do, but not the obvious thing where everyone's got the same sort of name. So you've got to have something that is unique to yourself. And it rolls off the tongue so that people remember it.

FREE LOCAL DELIVERY!

Credit
Facilities Available

SUITE SUCCESS
Manufacturers and retailers of furniture

With Compliments

Visit
Our Bed Showroom
On The First Floor

Longridge, Lancashire

PINEDEMONIUM INTERIORS

Emsworth, Hampshire

31

Penwortham, Lancashire

Hove, East Sussex

# British Hairways

Barber Shop — **BRITISH HAIRWAYS** — Walk in Service
Tel: 236 6922

FAST TAN SUNBEDS AVAILABLE HERE.

B. H. BARBER SHOP

B. H. BARBER SHOP

Barber Shop

**ANN PARKIN**

Millhouses, Sheffield

" *We used to have a barbers called 'A Close Shave'. Then we took over this salon. It was called something else. It had such a bad rep from the previous lot that we decided to completely change its name. And we went for British Hairways.* "

> *Going back about ten years ago, British Airways tried to sue us for using their name. They actually dropped it two days before it went to court. We've never heard anything from them since.*

It turned out that a rival reported us to BA's legal department. They thought they were doing us a bad turn, but they did us a favour. We ended up being in all the papers, TV and radio. If you didn't know the shop was here beforehand, you certainly did after.

**BRITISH HAIRWAYS**
British National Hairdressing Champion
LADIES & GENTS SALON
Tel: 0114 236 6922
987 Abbeydale Rd
Sheffield S7 2QD

Longridge, Lancashire

Tunbridge Wells, Kent

Islington, London

Great Barr, West Midlands

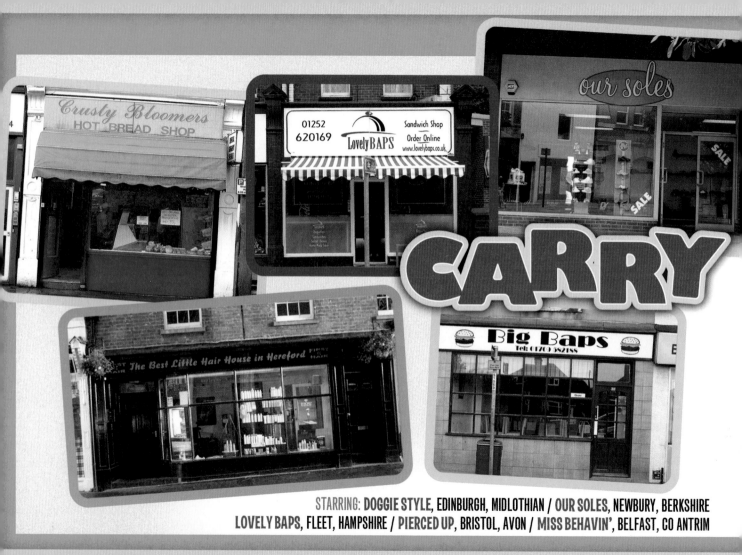

**CARRY**

STARRING: **DOGGIE STYLE**, EDINBURGH, MIDLOTHIAN / **OUR SOLES**, NEWBURY, BERKSHIRE
**LOVELY BAPS**, FLEET, HAMPSHIRE / **PIERCED UP**, BRISTOL, AVON / **MISS BEHAVIN'**, BELFAST, CO ANTRIM

Our search for the best in UK shop names has taken us to every corner of the country. This includes the dark, disturbing alleyways that are home to the seedier shops we have encountered. Although we find them distasteful, we are not prudes and we support your right to know our findings. So join us as Shop Horror takes you up the back passage of Britain's towns on a tour of *Risqué Retailers!!*

# ON SHOPPING

**BIG BAPS, SWINTON, SOUTH YORKSHIRE / CRUSTY BLOOMERS, CAMDEN, LONDON**
**THE BEST LITTLE HAIR HOUSE IN HEREFORD, HEREFORD, HEREFORDSHIRE / WET DREAMS WATERSPORTS, GYPSYVILLE, NORTH HUMBERSIDE**

Birkenhead, Merseyside

Leeds, West Yorkshire

Norwich, Norfolk

High Wycombe, Buckinghamshire

Warsash, Hampshire

Nether Edge, Sheffield

SHOE - BE - DO
SHOE REPAIRS · KEY CUTTING
BEACONSFIELD 5541 · CHESHAM 772318

Key
Cutting

ENGRAVING

Trophies
&
Tankards

**KARL ELLIS    JOHN ALDRIDGE**

Beaconsfield, Buckinghamshire

*I was lying in bed, trying to think of it. And I was singing to myself, badly. 'Shoobie-shoobie-do'. Then it came to me: 'Shoe-Be-Do'.*

48

PLEASE MAKE CHEQUES
PAYABLE TO
SHOE-BE-DO

*I set up the shop in 1981...or was it 1881? We've had cheques made out to Scooby Doo. I'm Scooby and he's Shaggy.*

What's-her-name from Birds of a Feather. Pauline Quirke? No the other one. She came in.

Val Doonican's wife, she's been a regular customer for years. What size feet? I couldn't tell you. A dainty size four. And that's just Mr Doonican.

People try other places, but they always come back. What brings them back? Just quality of work, we like to think.

Why do you get shoe repair and key cutting in the same place? We don't know. It's always been that way. There probably is a reason...but who knows?

GOGGLES ARE PROVIDED FOR YOUR PROTECTION & SAFETY

Norwich, Norfolk

Walkley, Sheffield

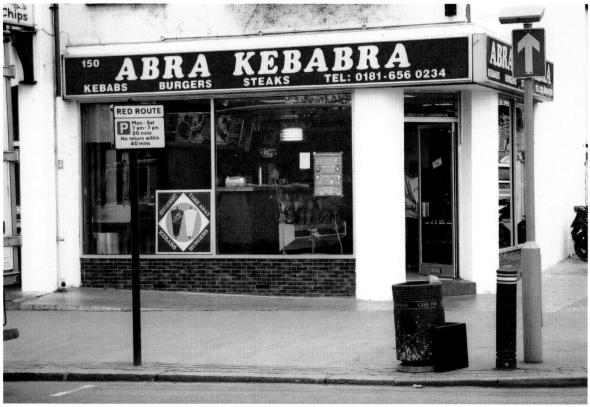

Shirley, Croydon

Hackney, London

**Walter Wall Carpets & Rugs**

Carpets    Vinyls    Quality Rugs    Natural Floorings    Fitting Service

**IAN HARRIS**

Yeovil, Somerset

"*The main one is, 'Can I speak to Walter please.' Or, 'Is Mr Wall there?' You tell people there's no such person and they're, 'No. I know him, I know him.' 'No, there really isn't such a person.'*"

*Axminster. That's the top. They do all kinds and none of it's cheap. I try to stay away from it really because as soon as you show a customer it they're like, 'Ooh that's expensive!' and they're out the shop before you know it.*

He doesn't make you work weekends. It's good hours and good money. Rob's my mate. He's working here just for the summer. We have a good laugh. Always something to do.

WALTER WALL CARPETS

Opening times

MONDAYS TO FRIDAYS
8.00AM – 5.00PM
SATURDAYS
9.00AM–5.00PM
SUNDAYS WE ARE CLOSED

Some people walk past and read it, second glance it and have a chuckle. 'Cos first of all, they're just like, 'Walter Wall' and they don't get it. Then they work it out and have a chuckle to themselves.

Broomhill, Sheffield

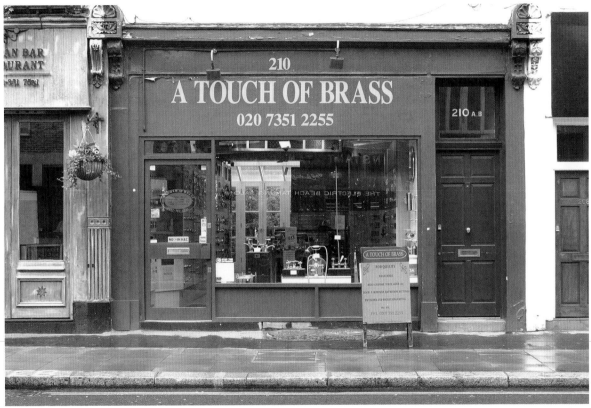

Fulham, London

Highbury, London

Oxford, Oxfordshire

59

After much discussion, we are still at a loss as to why these shops are named after 1980s pop acts. All we have concluded is that we like it so here is the Shop Horror top shop pop act chart.

BANANARAMA
TEL 449522 HIGH QUALITY FRUIT & VEGETABLES

Haircut One Hundred
Hair & Beauty Salon

shop of the pops

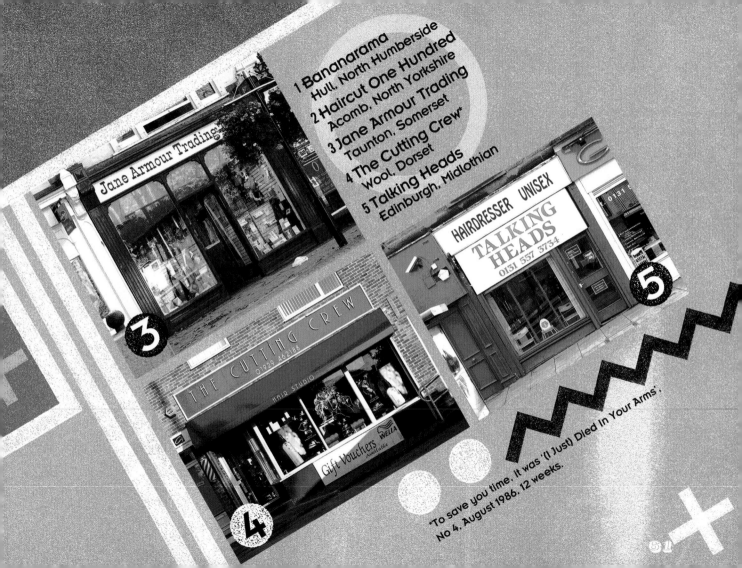

1 **Bananarama**
Hull, North Humberside

2 **Haircut One Hundred**
Acomb, North Yorkshire

3 **Jane Armour Trading**
Taunton, Somerset

4 **The Cutting Crew***
Wool, Dorset

5 **Talking Heads**
Edinburgh, Midlothian

*To save you time, it was '(I Just) Died In Your Arms',
No 4, August 1986, 12 weeks.

Wombwell, South Yorkshire

Shirley, West Midlands

Grantham, Lincolnshire

Clerkenwell, London

Grin n Wear it
Tattoo 'n' Piercing Studio
WWW.GRINNWEARIT.CO.UK TEL: 01842 861104

OPEN
10am–6pm

**RABBIT**

Lakenheath, Suffolk

*Getting a tattoo, that's the first thing that goes through your head: you've just got to grin and bear it. But I was thinking, you actually wear it.*

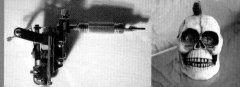

A client comes down from London once a month. He must be 70. He's having the full body suit. He's pretty much done now. He's only got a pair of socks to go.

If it's got skin on it, it can be tattooed. If you consider the armpit an unusual place, I've done armpits.

*The difference between tattooed people and non-tattooed people is that tattooed people don't care if you've got a tattoo or not.*

We numb the genitals so there's no sensation of the piercing... There's not a week goes by I don't do three or four.

The gun drives a needle under the skin, punctures through the first layer, and brushes into the second. That's where it leaves the pigment.

**STATE OF THE ART**

Tattoo Convention

This certificate is awarded to

*Rabbit*

on achieving

**1st Place**

in the category of

Most Unusual Concept – at convention

Probably the most common male piercing is a PA, which is a Prince Albert.

Leigh-on-Sea, Essex

Nether Edge, Sheffield

59

Ruddington, Nottinghamshire

Welcome To **Brighton** SHOP HORROR CAPITAL OF BRITAIN

The Royal Pavilion

Welcome to the WORLD FAMOUS **BRIGHTON PIER**

Welcome to **BRIGHTON PIER**

71

**BRIGHTON** is a town overflowing with civic pride. It is proud of its tourist industry. It is proud of its two universities. It is proud of its pier, its beach and the Royal Pavilion.

We too are proud of Brighton. But not for these reasons. We are proud because thorough research and analysis have shown that it has the highest concentration of amusingly named shops in the UK. Nowhere in the country has more gags per mile than this bold town. In London, you are never more than ten feet from a rat. In Brighton it is a funny shop sign.

Deputy council leader Sue John puts it down to the town's young and educated population: 'They're fun-loving types with a good collective sense of humour. Brightonians like a laugh and that's reflected in the shop names.'

It is also due to the high presence of that increasingly rare breed – the independent retailer. The town retains what is now a disproportionately large number of small shops. And these are the kind that like to indulge in naming fun.

For services to shop names and leading the way for the independent retailer, we are proud to officially declare Brighton the Shop Horror Capital of Britain.

Mr G Swillingham
Shop Horror
High Street
London

**BHCC**
BRIGHTON & HOVE
Chamber of Commerce

Dear Mr Swillingham

**Brighton shop names**

As one of the organisations representing businesses in Brighton, the Chamber of Commerce would like to thank you for rewarding the effort and thought that retailers have put into being different.

Having gone to the trouble of being witty in naming their businesses, I believe they will be very happy to have that recognised.

We are proud to accept this honour on their behalf.

Yours sincerely,

> **Thank you for rewarding the effort and thought that Brighton retailers have put into being different. Having gone to the trouble of being witty in naming their businesses, they will be very happy to have that recognised. We are proud to accept this honour on their behalf.**

JULIA STANFORD
SPOKESPERSON
BRIGHTON & HOVE CHAMBER OF COMMERCE

## Honourable mentions

**Brief Encounter** *Lingerie*
**EyeSite** *Optician*
**Deli'licious** *Delicatessen*
**Déjà Shoes** *Shoe shop*
**Food For Thought** *Café*
**Dig in the Ribs** *Restaurant*
**Heaven Scent** *Florist*
**The Plaice in the Square** *Fish & chips*
**Spaghetti Junction** *Restaurant*

### Brighton

SHOP HORROR CAPITAL OF BRITAIN

Hull, North Humberside

**ALAN KING**

Minehead, Somerset

"*I was going to call it 'Individuals', because my stock's quite different. And then it just dawned on me. 'Hang on a minute..."jewels". Why not put a "J" in there? That'll mean a lot more.' I'm quite good with words.*"

INDIVIJEWELS

EARRINGS WILL NOT BE EXCHANGED UNDER ANY CIRCUMSTANCES

One couple I remember particularly were on holiday. They came in and said, 'We really want to get our rings here because we love the name.' They bought them and then went out and took a picture of the shop too.

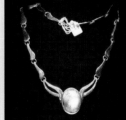

*The next name I was going to work on was 'Unujewels'. But it didn't quite work.*

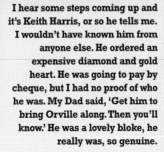

I hear some steps coming up and it's Keith Harris, or so he tells me. I wouldn't have known him from anyone else. He ordered an expensive diamond and gold heart. He was going to pay by cheque, but I had no proof of who he was. My Dad said, 'Get him to bring Orville along. Then you'll know.' He was a lovely bloke, he really was, so genuine.

Courtesy of
West Somerset Free Press

Forest Hill, London

Teddington, Middlesex

81

Edenbridge, Kent

Ainsdale, Merseyside

83

*Nearly-new Maternity Clothes And Dress-Hire*

www.DoesMyTumLookBigInThis.com

# OUT OF SITE

An amusing shop is the ultimate advert for a business, and a great source of entertainment for us. But spare a thought for those that have no shop. Very often small or emerging enterprises, they are deprived of this opportunity to speak to the world. More significantly, we are deprived of the chance to delight in their inventive names.

Shop Horror feels duty-bound to rectify that here. We present the greatest shop names that never were. We salute these budding businesses and look forward to the day they grow large enough to take their rightful place in High Street Britain.

Something For The Wickend

into your ...

Please carefully read any section relevant to your purchase.

Ear Candles

Candles

Magnotherapy & Magnetic Jewellery

Oil Bu

Home Fragrance

Magic Spell Boxes

Buy any 2 packs of and get a free

Aromatherapy Natural Hea Product

**Take-A-Fence**

Tel/fax:

L TYPES OF DOMESTIC, COMMERCIAL & SECURITY FENCING

**AKE - A - FENCE**

Supplied & Erected

Only The Highest Quality Materials Used Backed Up By Over 23 Years Experience In The Trade

FREE QUOTATIONS

**ALL WORK GUARANTEED INSURANCE WORK**

187 Sandhurst Road, Tunbridge Wells

**0189682323**

Mobile 07662 6621

Total price for

Yours sincerely,

09/05/04

**PLANET OF THE GRAPES**

MIKE BOOTH
WINE CONSULTANT

8 R

NOTT

PHON

EMAIL: michael.b

**Poultry In Motion**

**Docters Hill Farm**
**Docters Hill Lane**
**Hevingham**
**Norfolk**
**NR10 5NJ**

**SOCKET n SEE ELECTRICAL LTD**

Domestic / Commercial installations and repairs.
For free quotes call us on

**SOCKET N SEE ELECTRICAL LTD**

SPECIALISTS IN COMMERCIAL, DOMESTIC & MAINTENANCE

Mr.Gareth S

MOBILE 07772

ALL SCREWED UP

NUTS & BOLTS
SCREWS & FIXINGS
TEL: 0116 283 9900

Aylestone, Leicestershire

Southport, Merseyside

87

Herne Bay, Kent

Hove, East Sussex

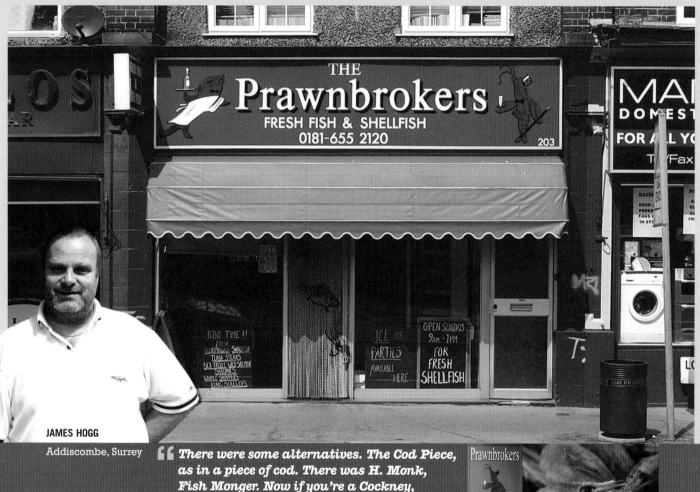

THE **Prawnbrokers**

FRESH FISH & SHELLFISH
0181-655 2120

203

BBQ TIME!!
FRESH
TIGER PRAWNS SWORDFISH
TUNA STEAKS
SEA TROUT WILD SALMON
SARDINES
WHOLE SNAPPERS
KING SCALLOPS

ICE FOR
PARTIES
AVAILABLE
HERE

OPEN SUNDAYS
9AM – 1PM
FOR
FRESH
SHELLFISH

OPEN

MA
DOMEST
FOR ALL YO

**JAMES HOGG**

Addiscombe, Surrey

" *There were some alternatives. The Cod Piece, as in a piece of cod. There was H. Monk, Fish Monger. Now if you're a Cockney, you'll know what that means.* "

Prawnbrokers

FRESH FISH
&
SHELLFISH

Peeled North Atlantic prawns and fish stock. £19.35. My wife has a recipe book. This will be shrimp soup, so I'm told.
**Alan Dufty,** customer

Two people pull up in car with a load of stolen jewellery. One turns to the other and shouts, 'It's a bloody fish shop' and drives off. I offered him some cod, but he didn't see the funny side.

The Rolls Royce of fish? Wild salmon, first day of the season. £25 a pound. I have a customer in Ascot who calls for it every year.

Ronnie Corbett asks for the biggest crab I've cooked. He knocks on the back door to collect it.

WHOLE
ROCK LOBSTER
TAILS
£9-90 EACH

*When people ask for prawns I say, 'Which would you like? We have over forty varieties.' See, I am a prawn broker.*

COOKED
CREVETTES
30/40 PER KILO
£17-99
BOX

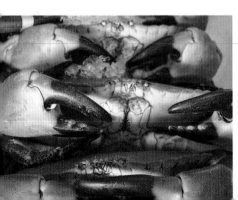

OPEN
BUSINESS HOURS

| | | |
|---|---|---|
| MONDAY | CLOSED A.M. CLOSED P.M. | |
| TUESDAY | 8·30 A.M.-5·00 P.M. | |
| WEDNESDAY | 8·30 A.M.-5·00 P.M. | |
| THURSDAY | 8·30 A.M.-5·00 P.M. | |
| FRIDAY | 8·30 A.M.-5·00 P.M. | |
| SATURDAY | 8·30 A.M.-5·00 P.M. | |
| SUNDAY | 9·00 A.M.- 1·00 P.M. | |
| LUNCH TIME | UNTIL | |

Prawnbrokers
FRESH FISH & SHELLFISH
James Hogg
203 LOWER ADDISCOMBE ROAD, CROYDO
TELEPHONE: 020 8655 2120

91

Stanstead Abbotts, Hertfordshire

Belfast, County Antrim

Teddington, Middlesex

SANDWICH AND COFFEE BAR

Lettuce Eat

Glasgow, Lanarkshire

**KNEAD THE DOUGH BAKERY**

**DIONNE MATHER    MAEVE WILLIAMS**

Llandeilo, Carmarthenshire

*"Is the shop's success related to the name? No, I don't think so. We're just nice people really. We do have a good laugh, yes."*

LARGE FRUIT TARTS £1·55

Naturally the bread goes best. We get a lot of the older generation. They like their teacakes and their sticky buns. They like the jam tarts too. They take them home to have with their tea.

*Occasionally they do come in and speak Welsh. I can get the gist of what they want. I'm from Portsmouth.*

AR AGOR
— OPEN —

Menter Bro Dinefwr
www.mentrau-iaith.com

Sometimes they come in and ask for something we haven't got. Nowadays people like rye bread. We don't do anything like that. A lot of people have this wheat intolerance now.

We get on well together because we're Capricorns. Capricorns get on with each other. I'm married to one as well. It's one of the few star signs that can get on with each other. Compatible, I think you call it.

382  Hair·O·Dyenamix  382
UNISEX SALON      020 8446 3373

FREE or FULL 1/2 HEAD | CUT AND BLOW DRY FOIL HI-LITES

OPEN SUNDAYS 10. TIL 4.0

380 Ballards Lane

380

North Finchley, London

Chorlton, Manchester

99

Wallingford, Oxfordshire

Ashford, Surrey

Failsworth, Manchester

Bronzi Beach

Unisex Tanning
Nail & Beauty Salon

Tel. 682 8220

BEAUTY

TANNING

Bradford, West Yorkshire

TAN TROPEZ

Unisex Tanning
Studio
024 7664 1885

OPENING HOURS

FIVE TEN-MINUTE TANNING SESSIONS
£10.00 !

FAST, HYGIENIC VERTICAL TANNING STUDIO

Nuneaton, Warwickshire

BEAUTY
THERAPY
WAXING · FACIALS
EYE TREATMENT

AWARD
WINNING
HIGH POWERED 180 XTRAS
COURSES AVAILABLE
VERTICAL TANNING UNITS

CREATIVE
NAILS
MANICURES · PEDICURES
NAIL PIERCING · ENHANCEMENTS

Tanz - in - Ere   Tel 626500

Beauty
Salon

The Very Latest in
Vertical Tanning Systems

2002

CREATIVE

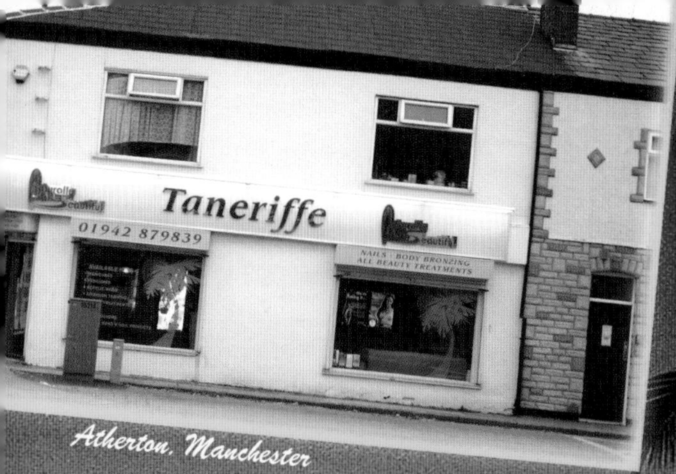

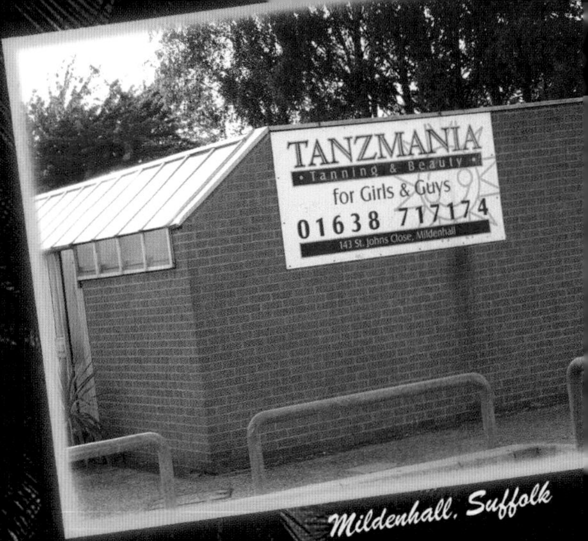

Taneriffe
01942 879839
NAILS · BODY BRONZING
ALL BEAUTY TREATMENTS

Atherton, Manchester

TANZMANIA
Tanning & Beauty
for Girls & Guys
01638 717174
143 St. Johns Close, Mildenhall

Mildenhall, Suffolk

# Tanfastic

**Why travel abroad this summer when a foreign destination can come to you, via your local neighbourhood tanning salon?**

Sunset photograph © Corbi

Waterloo, Merseyside

Bath, Avon

Bootle, Merseyside

Notting Hill, London

SNAKES 'N' ADDERS

Tel / Fax 0113 2899911

384

KIRKSTALL ROAD

SNAKES
TORTOISES
LIZARDS
TARANTULAS
CROCODILES
TURTLES

BOA / PYTHON
SPECIALIST

UV LIGHTS
VIVARIUMS
HEAT SYSTEMS
FROZEN FOOD
LIVE FOOD
BOARDING

· PIES · PASTIES ·
CURRIES · CHILLIES

Quality

At any time
No loading
at any time

**CHARLES THOMPSON**
Leeds, West Yorkshire

*I'm 23, this is my shop. I've been keeping them since I was 10. First bred them at 12. I used to work here at weekends. I was offered it. I went to the bank manager. Never looked back.*

☆ OPEN ☆
SNAKES
REPTILES
TORTOISES
LIZARDS
- VIVARIUMS -
ALL SIZES

DO NOT TOUCH THE GLASS.

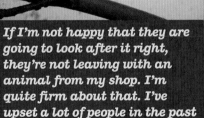

Most wanted? Probably the black-headed python from Australia. People love them. Or you can get albino forms of certain snakes that have colossal price-tags. Anywhere up to £10,000.

They're just so wonderful. The colours, the actions, the personalities that they show, the fact that they can constrict food, or kill food, or envenomate food, or all the different styles of protection.

They haven't got the brainpower to bond with you like a pet that you take for a walk. But they will get used to being handled without showing aversion to it. There's no likelihood of being bitten.

*If I'm not happy that they are going to look after it right, they're not leaving with an animal from my shop. I'm quite firm about that. I've upset a lot of people in the past who have come in.*

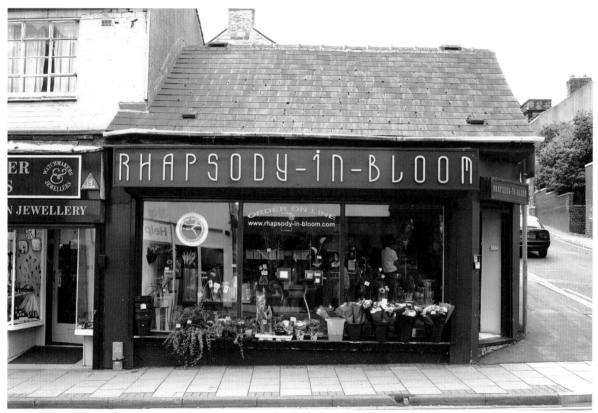

Barnsley, South Yorkshire

Roath, South Glamorgan

>Authentic Thai Food
:: take away

THAI
tanic

noodle bar<
eat in ::

Open

Belfast, County Antrim

Erdington, West Midlands

**Browned Off**

Tel: 01702 711778     Fax: 01702 713933

1619
Tanning,
Nails
& Beauty

HOLIDAY BRIDAL PACKAGES
200 WATT ULTRA FAST
TAN CABS
AIRBRUSH SPRAY TAN
MENS TREATMENTS
EYE TREATMENTS
GIFT VOUCHERS

NAILS    MAKE UP   WAXING
ACRYLIC    NAIL ART   FACIALS
UV GEL             MANICURE
CALGEL            PEDICURE
NSI GEL

**EUNICE BROCKMAN**

Leigh-On-Sea, Essex

" *I thought of when people say 'How are you?'
and you go 'I'm right browned off.' I wanted
something really ridiculous, so I chose that.
I'd had a few vodkas, mind.* "

It's everyone from the housewife to the courier girl to the youngsters to the grandmothers to the builder to the doorman to the bodybuilders on the men's side. We get a lot of the doorman bouncer types.

8. Use strengtheners/treatments ... and remember to have regular manicure...

Enjoy your new nails.

Browned Off.

How do you wax loose skin? You just make sure the fella holds it very tight. It's not very often. Not got that many brave blokes about at the moment, but they do have it done. 'Specially the body builders.

Browned Off
Tanning, Nails & Beauty

Price List

1619 London Road
Leigh-on-Sea
Essex SS9 3SQ

Tel. Shop: 01702 711778
Fax: 01702 713933

A member of the sunbed association

Anything unusual? What, like dyeing pubic hair and shaping into a heart on Valentine's day and dyeing it red and things? Loads of times.

*We were thinking of opening a chain: Browned Off, Cheesed Off, Pissed Off and F***** Off.*

Browned Off
New Company Category

NatWest

BROWNED OFF ACCEPTS NO RESPONSIBILITY FOR ARTICLES LEFT ON THE PREMISES. PLEASE MAKE SURE THAT YOU TAKE EVERYTHING WITH YOU.

Evening Echo

Swadlincote, Derbyshire

Edinburgh, Midlothian

Solihull, West Midlands

East Finchley, London

FAX:
0161
291
1077

Bits & Pieces Equestrian

Tel/Fax: 0161 969 4246

Open 'til 6:00 p.m. Wed. & Fri.

**SHAUN GREEN**

Sale, Cheshire

"*Who came up with it? I believe it were me. Just sat down and brainstormed. Me and Elaine. Bouncing names off each other over a couple of days. You get a few and keep coming back to one.*"

The 'bit' part is the steel bit that is attached to the bridle and goes in the horse's mouth. A 'piece' is an attachment on the bridle called the cheek piece, which connects the main bridle head part to the actual bit.

Do most people get the 'piece' part? Only them who've got horses who know how to take a bridle apart and put it back together know what a cheek piece is. Your normal man in the street definitely wouldn't know that.

*People say, 'Ooh that's good.' You know when you ring anybody up they go, 'Ooh that's ever so clever.'*

Southend-On-Sea, Essex

Willesden Green, London

Edinburgh, Midlothian

Dorchester, Dorset

If you thought 'TV shopping' meant orange Americans selling miracle cleaning products at the higher end of your satellite channels, let us correct you. Before Oxi Clean and Didi Seven, television shopping was a British tradition, and here we present its originators: High Street Britain's finest TV-based shop names.

# T.V. Shopping

Spex in the City

Covent Garden
London

Spex in the City
SightTools

**Hi-De-Hilites**
081-648 6439    Unisex Hair Salon

Mitcham
Surrey

**ALIAS QUIFF & COMBS**

Stoke-on-Trent
Staffordshire

**OPEN ALL FLOWERS**
01784 452300    01784 451780
www.openallflowers.co.uk

OPEN ALL FLOWERS

Staines
Surrey

**A PINE ROMANCE**
111    0181-361 5860

Friern Barnet
London

Godalming, Surrey

Halifax, West Yorkshire

**NORMAN D. LANDING**

MAIL ORDER
FILM & TV HIRE
MUSEUM SUPPLIES

MILITARIA **01202 521944**

76 ALMA ROAD WINTON, BOURNEMOUTH BH9 1AN

SPECIALISING IN
US ARMY CLOTHING
AND EQUIPMENT
1900 - 1945

**KENNETH LEWIS**
Winton, Dorset

*"'Can I speak to Norman?' or 'Mr Landing?'*
*That's what a lot of people ask for. I say*
*there's no such person. They find it hard to*
*believe sometimes. "*

I picked up a GI helmet in Normandy from a farmer who had been using it for a chicken-feed bowl. It's rusty, but it was used during the landings. Because of its history it's worth £1,500.

In *Saving Private Ryan*, at the beginning, when they hit the beach, Tom Hanks puts chewing gum on his bayonet and sticks a mirror on the end to see round a corner. Well that mirror came from here.

I sell American army uniforms and equipment from 1900 to 1945. It's for collectors and military vehicle owners who like to dress the part.

*I don't do German, I don't do weapons, and I don't do medals. It's only uniforms, equipment, and packaging like wartime cigarettes, sweets, and chewing gum.*

*The desirable items are tied to a famous person like Eisenhower. But I like the anonymous things.*

131

Consett, County Durham

Bilston, West Midlands

**MILLIONHAIRS** TEL. 653568 TEL. 653568

**ANDREW WALSH**
Norden, Rochdale

"I chose the name twenty years ago. I thought it was a good idea at the time. If I'd known sign-makers charge by the letter I'd have called it 'A1'."

SLUMBER NET
for day wear for night wear

Appointments

'Do you have to be a millionaire to come here?' I'm always getting that. Or, 'Are you a millionaire?' Not very likely, no.

*Thank you*
**for not**
**SMOKING**

It's a traditional, mature clientele. Predominantly ladies. We do do husbands as well. The ladies drag 'em in forcibly.

*We talk about everything that they say you shouldn't in a hairdressers: sex, drugs, religion, politics. Boob jobs. We talk a lot about boob jobs... and hip replacements.*

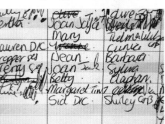

ANDREW'S
**MILLIONHAIRS**
NORDEN

796 EDENFIELD ROAD
NORDEN
Tel: 653568

HIGHLIGHTING
CUT-BLOW
PERMING, TINTING
NO SMOKING SALON

## MILLIONHAIRS

| | | |
|---|---|---|
| DRY TRIM | £ ... | 400 |
| SET BLOW | £5 | 50 |
| CUT & SET | £9 | 60 |
| CUT & BLOW | | 11.50 |

It's all regular customers. Each hour of each day of each week it's the same people that come in. It's a meeting place, a social event.

I've been coming here as long as Andrew's been here. Over twenty years. I was with him at his other place before.

**Sheila Smith,**
customer

TO ANDREW
CONGRATULATIONS ON YOUR
FIRST 25 YEARS

Kiveton Park, South Yorkshire

Ferryhill, County Durham

**NICK GAMBARDELLA**

Hove, East Sussex

"*Up north you buy beer and take it away. You call it a 'beer off'. So I thought, 'Burger Off'. It seemed to work. The local paper wrote, 'The name implies either the food is unfit or the customers are unwelcome.' There's no such thing as bad publicity…as long as you don't kill someone.*"

Lots of people know my chilli burger. I do mild, medium, hot, and painful. Customers bet with each other on whether they can eat it. Two fellas brought a girl in here. She was up for ninety quid and she almost did it.

**The odd fool now and again has chilli milkshake. Its taste? It takes your throat out, really nasty.**

The secret to a good burger? If I wanted to cut corners I could save £100 a week, but to me it's not worth it. I haven't put my prices up for three years.

*This used to be a dentist's. Sometimes little old ladies call up and I go 'Burger Off' and they go, 'Excuse me?'*

THIS IS NOT
BURGER KING
YOU DON'T GET IT
YOUR WAY.
YOU TAKE IT MY WAY,
OR YOU DON'T GET
THE DAMN THING.

**PRICES**
SUBJECT to CHANGE
ACCORDING TO
CUSTOMER'S
ATTITUDE

Three cheeseburgers for me, the wife, and sister. Can of Coke for the boy, two lots of chips. Been coming here about a year. I come about once a week. He knows what I want when I walk in the door.
**Derek Polling,** customer

SHAKES HOT CHILLI COFFEE
CHOCOLATE~BANANA
STRAWBERRY~VANILLA
BLACK CHERRY~LIME
MADE WITH SOFT ICE-CREAM.
VERTICOLD
RIGERATED DISPLAY    REFR

GARLIC
BREAD
4 SLICES £1·20

SPECIAL
KIDS MEAL

100% BEEF
PLAIN
CHEESE
ORIGINAL
BACON
CHILLI    MILD MEDIUM HOT XXX HOT
BLUE CHEESE
GARLIC
HAWAIIAN
CARIBBEAN
CALYPSO
MEXICAN
B-B-Q

# SAVE OUR SHOPS!

**Shopkeepers of Britain, your high street needs you!**
**Are you about to open a new shop?**
**Does your existing establishment need revitalising with a new sign?**

**Then we recommend a pun-based name!**

In business, you can never underestimate the importance of standing out from the crowd. We believe the best way to do this is with a humorous shop-front that engages and amuses your customers. It is guaranteed to be memorable and generate repeat custom.

Remember – you are not only improving your business, you are helping to keep High Street Britain a distinct and varied place.

Whatever your product, we encourage you to pick from these names we have created on your behalf.

Once you have selected an item from the list, please let us know. It could appear in the next edition of *SHOP HORROR.*

| | |
|---|---|
| SHOES | *The Shoe Must Go On* |
| WINDOWS | *Windows of Opportunity* |
| BIKES | *Bike to the Future, Bike to Basics, Cycle-logical* |
| GREENGROCERS | *Peter the Grape* |
| LOFTS | *Lofts in Space* |
| PRINTS & PAINTINGS | *Show Me the Monet* |
| THAI FOOD | *Old School Thai, Thai Me Up, Thai Me Down, Family Thais* |
| FISH & CHIPS | *Cod It Be Magic? Caught Between a Rock and a Hard Plaice, Pride of Plaice* |
| TOILETS | *At Your Convenience* |
| BEDS | *Simply Divan* |
| CURTAINS | *The Final Curtain, Pull Yourself Together* |
| HAIRDRESSING | *From Hair to Eternity* |
| INDIAN FOOD | *Curry Favour* |
| KITCHEN GOODS | *Here's Cooking At You* |
| WINE MERCHANTS | *Alexander the Grape* |
| SPORTS EQUIPMENT | *The Merchant of Tennis* |

IT IS WITH great regret that we announce the passing of the following Shop Horror establishments. Some have closed whilst others had their names changed. They no longer grace our High Streets, and these are poorer places without them.

Throughout their trading lives, they led the way in shop-name humour. Flying the flag of individualism and soldiering on in the face of dull name competition. They may not have won the fight, but they remained at their posts until the last item was sold. They served their High Streets well.

Their names are lost, but their memory lives on.

# R ✝ I ✝ P

## TAKIN' THE PIZZA

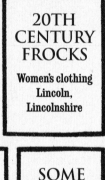

Pizza restaurant
Leeds,
West Yorkshire

## 20TH CENTURY FROCKS

Women's clothing
Lincoln,
Lincolnshire

## Special Award

The Shop Horror Special Award is given to an establishment that has shown excellence in name choice. It is awarded in recognition of flair, comic value, and originality in field of reference. This honour is being given posthumously to a florist in Portslade, East Sussex. The award goes to . . .

## BACK TO THE FUCHSIA

We hope some day that someone will follow their lead and open the sequel: Back to the Fuchsia II.

## TAN-GERINE

Tanning, Bradford,
West Yorkshire

## SHADY LADY

Lighting, Walkden,
Manchester

## THE BOARDROOM

Snowboarding equipment, Brighton, East Sussex

 ## DECKADANCE

Records, Canterbury, Kent

## NAPOLEON BOILER PARTS

Plumbing supplies, Midhurst, West Sussex

## BLOOMIN' WONDERFUL

Florist
Uxbridge,
Middlesex

## SOME PLAICE ELSE

Fish and chips
St Albans,
Hertfordshire

# JOIN THE HUNT

The shops in this book represent the best of the worst of those that have been discovered so far. However, more are out there. They may be newly opened businesses or existing ones that have managed to escape our notice.

Shop Horror is a continuing quest to seek out these extra stores, note their existence, and preserve their image for posterity. You can help. Throughout the UK, growing numbers of shop-spotters are trawling the streets. This is your opportunity to join them. Put on your anorak, load your camera, and start spotting in the name of Shop Horror. When you find an amusing store, send us the details using this form. The best will appear in the next edition of the book.

*NAME OF SHOP*

*TYPE OF SHOP*

*SHOP ADDRESS*

*POST CODE*

*PHONE NUMBER*

*YOUR NAME*

*YOUR ADDRESS*

*YOUR PHONE NUMBER*                    *YOUR EMAIL ADDRESS*

*SEND TO: Shop Horror c/o Fourth Estate, 77–85 Fulham Palace Road, London W6 8JB or email suggestions@shophorror.co.uk*